To the Borders of Light

Poems

Sharon K Sheppard

for
Bruce, Kate, Eva, and Ella

Also by Sharon K Sheppard
All We Ever Wanted © 2013
As If It Were Visible © 2014

Table of Contents

Acknowledgements

Many thanks to friend and fellow poet Dave Healy, to whom I have now entrusted three books. Without his expertise, I am sure I would still be contemplating, rather than publishing, a book.

Thanks to all who have commented to me about poems that you particularly enjoyed. You remain my strongest incentive for sharing my poetry.

Thanks to family and friends, who continue to be the heart of my life. Without you, there would be precious little to write about.

"Friend, if thou wilt be something, stand not still:
Thou must from one light to another go."

~Angelus Silesius

Introduction

I wake every morning around 5:30 am. No alarm clock is needed except the one in my head, which has been timed over the years to the feeding of children, an hour-long drive to work, and now, in retirement, the simple pleasure of watching the sun come up. Each morning I think about the long string of days and nights that has been mine. How did it happen that I had this particular life? Much of it was surely the result of choices I made, but a great deal came by simply moving from one day to the next. There is a certain wisdom to be gained by simply living, by going from one light to another.

When I write, I am conscious of how life weaves one day into the next until finally we stand at the far end of a lifetime, wondering where the time has gone. Much of our experience remains locked inside. We are treasure troves of such. But some of it can be shared in one way or another. Poetry is my way of sharing. For me, poetry captures those moments in which I am most myself, or at least most who I want to be.

It is my hope that those who read these poems will see something of themselves here, and will sense, in reading them, permission to share themselves, too, in a world that clearly needs us all.

To the Borders of Light

Poems

So Envious

The old red barn is falling slowly
toward the pond,
leaning more steeply every year,
conceding its long usefulness
to the inevitable. In the mirrored surface
of the water, a second barn falls
slowly upward. One bright day, or perhaps
one dark night, the two will surely
collapse into each other
with something akin to an irresistible love.
If only I could be there to watch,
so envious
from the shore.

Lake Francis

Late afternoon,
and some kindled fire
pours a pale scrim of smoke
across Lake Francis, where it hangs
brooding above the water,
contemplating the sorrow
of its own dissolution.
All of autumn shimmers
in the lake's expansive mirror;
clouds skimming its blue glass surface,
tree tops, leaping up like fire!
If only I could rise
from these heavy shoes,
sprout wings, and fly across it.
I would trail my open hand
in that coolness,
part the taut barriers of air and water,
and unravel those phantom trees
into light, their rippled branches
touching me like hands,
peeling down
every mundane mask
I hide behind.

Inevitability

Summer, with its
warm rains and soft nights,
its joining of bodies and births,
has vanished entirely
into the gray-brown husk of autumn.

Emptiness expands
into the fields
like silence pours
its long, lonely body
into an abandoned house.

Life retreats.

We sadden, and regret
our inattention. Even
the smallest soulful creature
grows wise
with inevitability.

Solo

Behold!
One cricket
pours its longing
into night,
that fragile blue cup
with stars
along the rim.

Whatever Geese

The cold has come again. Faintly,
through closed doors and windows,
comes the barking of geese
migrating in the pale morning sky.
I imagine how they bank above my house,
their wings ticking like feathered metronomes,
then ripple across my neighbor's rooftop
like a tattered gray ribbon, and fade
into distance. All of this, I perceive
in an instant, as vividly as if I had
seen, as-well-as heard it.
Three tiny bones vibrate
against the tympanic membrane
of my eardrum, sparking to life
whatever geese reside inside my head.
They rise on dark wings,
trailing gray against the sky.
Winter's breath rides their tails
like a white fire!

Oak Wilt

One by one, they go,
The slick green promise of leaves
Choked thin.

Defeated trunks loom now
Like the masts of ghost ships
Abandoned to wind.

Where are the generations of rain
That raised them up, cell by cell
Year by year?

Where are the lost summers
Of robins warbling
From their leafy heights?

By their reaching, our lives
Were measured out, as surely
As if we, too, had sprouted

And pushed our way up
Through layers of crumbling leaves
And down, into groundwater.

There are deep connections
In this world,
Between one life and another,

And invisible griefs
Passed, root-to-root
Beneath the surface.

One day you waken, as from a dream,
And find that life
Has irretrievably changed.

Chip Pile

This alone remains
Of fifty years' greening span,
Of shouldering-up through drought and rain,
Of wrestling with the wind:
Every inch of woodsome gain,
Fall-flamed and winter-bit,
Within a single season's pain
Laid low, undone by human hands,
Now humbled, broken, slain.

November

Little by little,
summer's green ocean
heaves its dying colors
onto the drab shores of November.

The wind croons its dry psalms
in the brittle fields, and light contracts
as the prow of our mutinied ship
turns toward darkness.

All of the grief-salted tears
in the world
cannot stop it.

What We Deign To Start

One does not question time's relentless march,
But turns the bleakness over into hope
By folding daffodils into the slope
Of sandy soil soon bit by winter's parch.
How patiently they rest beneath the arch
Of hillside, as we humans strive to cope
With cold and darkness, winter's icy grope
And chill. But springtime's fulsome frill and starch,
The slow unfolding brightness 'neath the hill,
Undoes the grip of ice upon the heart,
For in its secret places, no night's chill
Might ever kill the dream of spring, nor halt
The yellow yearnings of the daffodil
To finish boldly what we deign to start.

Gone

Colors that danced
along the ruffled shoulders
of the trees
have gone now, and the world
is turning over once again,
becoming brown
and drab,
and shuffling off to sleep.
The empty branches
seem so bare, so full of
somber expectation.

How calmly
they await the muffled glories
of the snow.

Fishing

Undone by snow, its utter white
I cast my lot with sleep,
And dreamt I angled through the night
For poems, in the deep.

No touch of ice to numb me there,
No wintry wind to blow.
I sat and pondered how to snare
Some eloquence below.

No scaly rainbowed word appeared
To titillate my mind,
But something dark, a shadowed fear
Rose up. What if I find

No elegance, no silvered fish,
No delicate white flesh,
But something common as a dish
Flip-flopping in my nets?

I shook it off, cast one more line
Into the wordy sog;
Released myself from the sublime,
And caught this humble frog.

Evidence

Whose scrabbled tracks across the snow
Belie a world in thrall to cold;
Call into question all we know
Of winter's grip, its icy hold?
Some furred or feathered beastie, bold
Has left its scribbled nibbling mark
O'er every blinding swale and fold
Of unrelenting whiteness stark.

Christmas Enough
for Eva

Mirrored
in the reflective glass
of this crowded airport terminal,
the ghostly gray bodies
of weary travelers
walk into and through
each other,
without recognition.

Soon
I too, will place blind faith
in concepts of thrust and lift,
and hurtle across the snow-crusted
face of America, suspended
for a few brief hours
between one frantic Christmas
and another.

This is a far cry
from Bethlehem's star-filled skies
and that other travel-weary family,
doing what good families do
to keep their children
warm and fed and protected
until destiny's hand sweeps them
toward an unknown future.

14

Only last night you lay
in a sleepy heap across my shoulder,
your sweet baby head
resting damp and downy
against my cheek. Miraculously,
time stepped aside for the moment
and waited for *us*. That, baby girl
was Christmas enough for me.

Interplay

Outside
in the darkness,
snowdrifts nudge one another,
sidling up
to the patio window,
casting small fistfuls of ice
against the glass.

Inside, two sixty-watt bulbs
throw back a swath
of pale light, illuminating
the surface of snow
and creating, of their interplay
a landscape
of mountains, valleys, and craters.

Not far
from where I sit,
the fragile blue light
drops off into infinity.
How lonely it must be
on the dark side
of the moon.

Ornamental

Breathe in the murmurings
of what you love.

The face of the tiny glass Santa,
its shine rubbed away
by years of handling,
by shufflings into and out of boxes,
by long hibernations in
the dark silence of closets, and cameos
on the prickly, pine-scented stage
of Christmas
                    glows now, with age
the way old people glow
with their long years of usefulness.

What whispers, then, from this old friend?

Hang in there.
Someone may yet come
to recognize the beauty of your scars,
the rich patina of authenticity
in your tarnished body.

After Christmas

One by one, I gather in
Their brittle treasure, lately hung
From piney boughs, whose arms wide-flung
Upheld them, gently. Through the din
Of all our joyful Christmas-ing,
That quiet circle, every night,
Bespoke the peace I felt within
Remembering the Savior's light.

January

January's shoulders
Stiffen, creak, grow older.
She stoops beneath the burden
Of snow's accumulation,
(Its sifting scintillation)
And draws a frosty curtain
O'er every hill and dale,
Casts far her icy veil
'Til cold alone is certain.

Whatever Infinity

Through steep winter,
like old bones stacked
against the bitter blaze of white,
the oak stands firm in one thing.
Spring, with its warm arms, will come.
Life, the unstoppable
will once again
shake fire
from its branches. This
is the expected miracle, the one
we all count on. Like clockwork,
beyond any hope of comprehension,
we entrust ourselves
to the repetitive motion
of a spinning planet in thrall
to a burning star.
Light ebbs, then returns, as from a vast sea.
Something not unlike love, stirs
within the heart of the tree.
Sap rises. Ice-bitten buds open
into flowers, then leaves.
Heedless of age, or time
or any expectation
of death,
it begins once more
to pour its mortal body into

whatever infinity it has been granted,
be it armfuls of snow
or the reaching transparent roots
of water.

A Secret Grief

One day, I finally notice
how the red and green leaves
of the poinsettia
have curled, and crisped
and fallen silently away,
floating soundlessly
to the floor like a secret grief.
How unobtrusive
death is,
passing its cool dry hand
over us,
leaving nothing
but parched remnants
of the blood-red life
we remember.

Gleam

After the snow
Unfolded its quiet blanket,
One by one
The silent stars came out.

A full blue moon,
Pale and shining as
A great round bird, nestled
Into the frost-tipped branches.

And nothing
Seemed certain
But the light.

Lucy

She fits
　perfectly
into the crook
of her grandmother's arms,
sleepy head pillowed
against a life forever widening
　to contain her.
What clues to this life
　does she gather?
A voice, lit with laughter.
A smile, warm as welcome.
Hands, ready to soothe
　and smooth her fears.

A heart, opening wide
　to embrace
whoever she becomes.

This

What is a human being?
This. A spirit clothed
in presence and perspective,
gifts we all possess.

Easy to believe
that I am the center,
a lone island
upon whose shores
the entire Universe washes
in great tides of experience.
But look! A secret to be revealed!
The Universe is balanced
intricately
on the presence and perspective
of all. And I, like a tuning fork,
hum unbidden
with music I did not write.

Gravitation

How easy it finally is
to be separate,
conveniently forgetting
how every molecule moves,
bumping shoulders with the rest.
Though, to be sure
a few gravitate greedily
to one soul, or another.
Whether to stand
on the inside, or out?
In this world,
we may go where we will,
but few do.

Kate of the Two Hearts

At ten, she carries them,
one resting against each
blue-jeaned hip.

In her right pocket, a heart
of stone . . . smooth, and weighty
with dreams as yet undreamt.

In her left pocket, a heart
of threaded glass, open-yet-fragile,
light-filled, and sure to break.

They warm to the slow tick of girl
toward woman, the knitting-together
of bones with purpose.

And she carries them lightly,
without contradiction, as the waiting world
prepares its welcome.

My Hairdresser

She seats me comfy in a chair,
Runs all her fingers through my hair,
Then parts, and combs it to one side,
(the tangles taken in her stride)
While I sit back, without a care.

"I'll make you beautiful!" she cries,
As comb teeth rake across my eyes.
And though I know she'll make the most
Of what I've got, my 'do' is toast
Along with makeup's thin disguise.

She twists me, turns me, leans me back
Like some poor sinner on the rack;
Braids me, frays me, gathers my strands
Into a noose of rubber bands,
And just as I'm about to crack,

Says with a flourish, that she's done,
Remarks, "Oh, grandma! That was fun!"
And lifts the mirror to my face.
Although my hair is a disgrace
From which a mangy dog might run,

She's rid me of my foolish pride,
Unmasked the age I tried to hide.
And now I'm who I'm meant to be,
A rag-doll grandma, happily
Un-coiffed, redone, and beautified.

Grandpa

The cavern of his hand,
Its gentle time-worn span,
Deftly blunts your baby tears,
Uplifts you, eye-to-eye,
Soothes every fretful cry.
He who rubs bright sparks of cheer
Into your tousled head,
Elicits smiles instead,
Conjures laughter from your fear.

Elegy for Cookie Grandma

You exited, stage right
About the time I stepped out into life,
When love in all its dizzying dimensions
Had found me.

Your last words, from the hospital
And over the phone, were this:
"I can't die. Only good people die."
And that, was simply that.

I squirmed for years beneath the weight
Of this well-intentioned humor.
You were the grandma who holed up
In her tiny upstairs apartment,

One day looking much like another,
Sandwiched between mornings in bed
With "True Detective", and evenings
In front of the TV with Perry Como.

You were the grandma of housedress and slippers,
Of long gray hair, twisted into a bun at your neck,
Whose half-deafness was only half-solved
By the unwieldy hearing aid clipped to your dress

And the strident efforts of those who loved you.
Somehow, you had launched five children
Out of the ruins of a husband's suicide,
Every last one of them diligent and kind.

But for us, your cookies marked you best:
That clown-shaped jar in the kitchen corner
With oatmeal-raisins cached in its belly
Like so many nuggets of chewy gold.

For them, you attained, and bore well
The name of Cookie Grandma.

All these years later, their wafted cinnamon
Still whispers your goodness,
Who guaranteed to her children's children
The right of love by-way-of-cookie;

Who cackled through toothless gums,
And bore the weight of her many years
With humor, and not a little imagination,
Snatched from the arms of death.

We Were a Circle

We were a circle then,
all elbows and impatience
as we waited around the
white Formica tabletop
for the muffled pop-popping of corn
from the cast iron kettle.
We made a tablecloth between us
of last week's *Sac City Sun,* and
leaned into the lettered patchwork
of its small town news, grain market prices,
  and obituaries.
We were a circle, and 'kitchen'
was just one more word for happiness.
Grandma poured us milk,
and Grandpa shook that kettle hard
over the stove's hot blue flame.
When at last it had quieted,
he lifted it in age-freckled hands,
and poured the fragrant white mountain
amongst us, where we gobbled it,
(steamy, and crisped with salt)
printer's ink, and all.

Standing at the Settler's Graves
  a sonnet for the unnamed dead

Whose umber bones beneath this mountain's breast
Define these lichened stones, upturned and gray,
Now stained by rain and time, now worn away?
Who were they, those who take their humble rest
Inside an unfenced, unplowed plot of soil
Well-dug by kin, by those who loved them best,
While unmarked headstones stand the final test
Of time, but leave their places nameless, all?
We pause beneath an ancient flag of sky
Whose azure depths, today, shine no less blue,
To ponder how their struggles, toil, and tears
More worthily than words, identify
The journey of these unsung, unnamed few
Entombed within this hill so many years.

A Little Hardship

There is a longing
For my higher self
Persistently pecking within this shell,
But I cannot rise
From the sticky bed of comfort.
Hardship creates necessity.
Necessity, action.
I could hope
For a little hardship.

Poem To Myself

You! Struggler!

Drive a stake
Into the swirling chaos!
Find yourself a chair and sit
At the center.

Decide one thing.
Believe one thing.
Achieve one thing.
Be one thing.

Life is as simple as that.

Definitions

so many words lying
about tripping us up telling us
what we are what we
aren't what we ought to be
what we might be
if only

words into which
we pour
every holy thing

supposing
we swept them beneath the rug
cast them into darkness
snapped our perfect fingers
unburdening
the crooked-yearning-to-be-straight
the perennially unwise   the child
in its mother's arms
still rocking to the freedom
of its own definition

what remained
might well resemble
an honest conversation
with God

Welcome

Wrapped
in the defining layers
of Muslim womanhood,
she inhabits, rather than sits in
a single aisle seat, and stares
through a veil of memories
rich with experiences for which
I have no reference, or understanding.
Still, we are both female, and bear
in our bodies the ever-unfolding potential for life
with its twin pregnancies of sorrow, and love.
I ponder that, as the jet-hum lulls me to sleep.
Half-a-country later, at the Baggage Claim in St. Paul,
it seems the entire Somali clan has come
to wrap her in its arms and kiss her.
Over and over, through tears, they pat her cheeks
and whisper words of reassurance.
Finally, exhausted by long travel,
she slumps into the chair next to mine.
Something unutterably human
compels me to add my tears
to theirs. I reach into
the wordless space between us,
touch her gently, and say,
"Welcome."

Silence

Sometimes, I have
the saddest meditations
on silence…how it fills up the spaces
between us, but refuses to mean anything,
or be anything. I try to pin it down, but it is
nowhere to be found. I try to fill it up, but
it absorbs my every word. I try not to
listen to it, but it shouts at me
out of the depths of your absence.
Sometimes I am so lonely for you.
Please come, and fill the empty silence
with your love.

Forget-me-nots

Forget-me-nots
in their tiny silk dresses,
spark blue
against the brown crumble
of old leaves. Dancing
among the slender new wisps
of grass, they twinkle
like stars,
rising wistfully into
a season
they cannot survive.

Frail,
yet unforgettable,
their brightness lingers
within us
long after dust
has claimed their form.

In This Space

In this space
with its hallways and hungers,
its walls forever folding and collapsing
  without warning,
  out of season,
there are eyes that braid
the faintest of lights
into a redefinition of sight,
hands that open without taking,
words that arrive among us
rich with gifts.

Evangeline

When you turned at last
and walked into those arms of Light,
I thought how often your life
had been rent by pain, and how
you always waited
for love to ply its careful needle
and mend the tear. Some days, the light
of your faith, shining behind your eyes,
made you so beautiful I could only wonder
at your quiet unawareness
of how it lifted others up.
We were given, like babes, into your hands
and you held us all so gently.

Visiting Evelyn

She slides downhill,
a little every day, like a glacier
clinging to a mountainside. Soon,
some salty sea will claim her.
But not today.

Today she sits and smoothes
the work-worn surface of the
kitchen table with her hand.
Just behind her eyes, memory
stirs like a fluttering sparrow.

She tells how the table was found
years ago, in a chicken house,
and pressed into service. Then
she rises from her chair, out of habit
to fetch us a little food, or some tea.

We have all just eaten,
and those who love her say,
"No ma. It's fine. Sit down."
She sits then, and resumes
the story of the table.

Married at fourteen,
she dropped five children
through her body and into the world.
All but one sweet daughter
grew up to call her blessed.

I imagine them gathered
around this table, as she cooked
and coddled and cared for them
down the years. Now, it is they
who care for her.

She is so happy we have come.
Her eyes seem beautiful
with the light of simple kindness.
"Are you hungry?" she asks,
and rises again, out of habit.

I have an impulse to touch her face.
To coax back
that fluttering sparrow
lest it fall, and disappear forever
beneath the waves.

Green Army Men

On rainy days,
you would line them up in regiments
across your unmade bed,
sheets and spread scrunched up
into hills and valleys, towns and territories.
Sometimes, our big cat Fluff
would leap into their midst, and morph himself
into a gray purring no-man's land.

You had learned, as young boys do,
to ape the boom of cannons, and spit out
the ut-ut-ut of machine gun fire.
You were "The General,"
    Patton, in a red striped T-shirt.
With a sweep of your hand
enemies fell, never to rise again.

Years later,
when real life came for us,
we would succumb to it,
    each in our own way.
But for those few years, in the
tangled trenches of an unmade bed,
you were god-like, unshakable,
your authority beyond question.

The Find

It rests on the tabletop
for many days, and I visit it often,
for it is as beguiling as
a secret sin. When I pass by
it whispers to me, as it first did
from the long white table
at the sale. I know
I will eventually box it up,
and stow it away
with all of my other faded loves.
But for now, it is my darling,
my sweet find…the very heart
of my unrepentant self.

To my grandmother, who died when I was ten

You flutter up sometimes
out of distance,
                    like leaves caught
by wind, prick the silence.

Grandmother. Kentucky-born.
Shaper of loaves, and children,
                    lover of bold hats
pinned into Sunday morning hair.

Your blue-veined hands
still reach for red
amid the green tangle of years,
                    pulling me

into a deep remembering
                    sweet as the roses
you tied against the house,
a beguilement to passing bees.

Grandmother, if you will forgive me,
  I will forgive you.

You could not stay for my woman-ing
and I, unable to hold it back,
                    left you behind.

Now, I stake my own claims
in gardens, and grandchildren,
in red days that open and close,
                              a turning of pages
by hands that look like yours.

A Hat Such As

It is a hat such as
coquetterie demands,
a fuschia-feathered razzmatazz
form-fitting to the pate
of one who radiates pizazz,
whose jeweled Flapper fingers snugged
it tightly down, whereas
she neither feared to rise and dance,
nor shake her stuff to "all that jazz."

Can It Be

What I treasure today
must soon be left behind:
all of the coveted and acquired
   trappings of a lifetime,
that I might step out, bodiless
into the next thing. Imagine
the relief of it! Can it be
that this disrobing of flesh
   and possessions
is something that I long for?

Pale Blue Morning

In the somber blue light,
what is left
  of pale snow,
  of its tired blue scatter
peels away,
molecule after molecule,
into the pale blue air. Sylphlike,
from the open palm of February,
it tingles, and rises,
then disappears
into the chill of morning.
  And who can say
whether this fading away
into nothing
is a kind of death,
or a resurrection?

Abandoned Barn

Through years of summer's bake, and winter's bite
Its ruddy, rough-sawn sides stood straight and tall.
Beneath the hay-sweet dimness of its height
Two horses blew and nickered. Pigeons called.
The farmer came to open it each dawn,
To let some sunlight in, some darkness out,
To fork down fragrant hay into the stall
And ponder what this strange old world's about.
But now it leans and creaks, and there's no doubt
That usefulness has nearly run its race,
For no one comes to let the darkness out;
Within its musty walls remains no trace
Of horse or hay...but pigeons strut, and grime
Its crumbling rafters, white-washed now, by time.

To Make a Point

Like a spent tsunami,
what remains of snow and ice
has withdrawn from ditch
and yard. In its wake, our pasts
come back to haunt us: rusting
overturned bike, the car that died
in early Fall, scattered runes
of plastic and aluminum,
the alternating fluff and sog
of disintegrating newspaper.
What careless beast can have
passed this way, shrugging off
these shaggy disasters?

Spring is nothing, if not forthright.
First she disrobes us, and then
as if to make a point,
turns up the heat and light.

Jitterbugging

Curled, like a small white cat
at the foot of the oak,
the last patch of grit-laden snow
hunkers down in the dismal rain.

From the neighbor's yard,
blue jays and crows blare obscenities
at each other, and the world would seem
callous and cold, but for this:

Jitterbugging, along the flank
of one rain-streaked tree,
a nuthatch hangs upside down,
just to prove he can.

Even If

Surely, today
there will be rain.
Yesterday's scattered seed
will swell and crack.
The chickadees will not
carry it away in their beaks, laughing.

It will grow.

Where the drab gray dust now reigns,
slender green wisps will rise.
Crickets will sing
among its flowering stalks.
Deer will bow down in it.
Chipmunks will hide from hawks
in its soft whorls and swales.
And all will be right again
with the world, even if
I cannot live forever.

Remind Me

At last
the rain has come,
and where it pools,
a mirror
in which one joy
or another, is replicated.
By its shine, O God
remind me
of your infinite pathways
to love.

A Corner

I dreamt that I explained, carefully
to a total stranger,
the delicately shaded meaning
of the word 'corner';
that a corner is more than
a catch-all for dust, or a dead-end,
but can also be a place
from which escape is possible,
a place from which to envision
and execute one's life,
a turning point
from which to set out
in a new direction.

It all seemed perfectly clear, and simple.

But when I woke, the stranger
was gone, and life
had resumed its usual dimensions
   and definitions.
                        A corner
was back to being a place
you arrive at easily,
but leave
with great difficulty.

The Perfect Shot

All that is required
are a steady hand, and a
good sense of timing. That
and the immense mechanics
of a turning planet, the dependable
cameo appearance of our nearest star,
and a few soft clouds fingering up
at the horizon. It helps
if there is an ocean, full of motion and foam,
and a sleepy morning sky, just waking
to its own pink and purple reflection.
Still, there are always surprises.
Consider yourself lucky
    if, at the last instant
a lone sea gull glides
into the captured heartbeat
of your frame.

Five Black Ducks

Five black ducks
floating
beyond the breakers;
lost, yet not lost
in the gray immensity
of morning.

Shell

Little spiral staircase
in my pocket,
turning . . . turning
round the sea salt
life-without-eyes
that made, of its own secretions
a home, an intention,
a center.

The Wave

It arrives
as from a long journey,
lifting its petticoats of foam
then spreading them out
across the sand
where, gingerly, a sea gull
steps over them
into the other world.

Dogs On the Beach

Their paw prints tell the tale
of how they run in joyous circles,
into and out of the waves, scattering
plovers and sea gulls to the wind,
snuffling at whatever the night's gray tide
has carried in, until at last,
called back by beloved masters,
they return
in tongue-lolling, ear-flopping
exhaustion,
their wet black noses
grainy with sand.

High Tide

Do not be fooled.
Whatever it was
that beguiled your eye
with its color, shape, or shine;
whatever you passed by
on your way
to somewhere else;
it will not be there
when you return.

Pelicans

Pelicans
in tight formation,
carefully spaced,
wings pumping in unison,
glide through morning fog,
barely brushing the waves.
Gullets tucked in,
landing gear up and secured,
they fly low, beneath radar,
just in case.

Sea Foam

Little halos, little necklaces of foam
framing, and softening
what the tide has abandoned,
all of the unhallowed dead
along the shore.
  Barnacled crab.
  Sand dollar.
  Flotsam of bone or wood.
Every washed-up thing,
embroidered
with a fretwork of airy pearls,
so frail that the shine of them
endures but minutes,
  then disappears
  into nothing
like the pale distant points
of stars, winking out.

Two Horseshoe Crabs

On the beach,
two horseshoe crabs
locked in an embrace.
Even after all those eons
of evolution, life
still comes down to this:
One body yearning
for another.

Salt, calling to salt.

If the sea came now
with its cold gray arms,
what could I do
but surrender?

Low Tide

1

At low tide, the beach
is a moonscape of craters
and undulations. Everything
spit out by the waves and left behind
casts a long blue shadow.

2

What is broken remains broken.

3

Still, I bend
to right a struggling crab
whose hideous legs claw air.
Why have the gulls not yet found him?
He wastes this chance to escape,
and waits calmly
for the incoming tide to save him.

4

Stupid crab . . .

5

I think
if I could find one
whole, perfect thing here
I might be satisfied.

6

Some days, I feel almost invisible.

7

Down the beach
a sea gull,
perfectly happy to be a sea gull,
stands ankle-deep
in the blinding glare of sunrise.

Great Blue Heron

Had you been pink,
I might have mistaken you
for one of those plastic flamingos
once ubiquitous in gardens.
But in sunset's long afterglow,
you are neither pink, nor
the steely blue-on-gray one expects.
You are mystery walking.
A tall, needle-nosed stalker
who slowly lifts the pitchfork
of one foot, sets it into the muck,
and then, with equal care
lifts, and sets down the other.
Once or twice, you stab out
with the long stiletto of your beak.
Then, you tip one moon-dark eye
in my direction, and like
a Zen master cloaked in feathers,
you dismiss me.

There is little I can do
but snip the bright thread of my attention,
gather up this happiness,
and go home.

Benediction

Late afternoon, and a paper-thin moon
melts onto the blue tongue of the sky
like a half-consumed communion wafer.

I can't help but wonder who left it there,
pale and half bitten-through,
heedless of admonitions it might bleed.

It does not bleed . . . but brightens
as blue deepens into night. And isn't
this also a sign of God's grace to us?

Host of consecrated light, lifted up
night after night,
pronouncing its pale benediction.

Four Swans

Four
Swans
Floating
Like blossoms
Against the green day
One dreaming, head beneath her wing
Another gliding like a ghost in the mirrored sky
The third, still as the morning star
Watching, as the fourth
Unfurls its
White wings
To
Fly

Thinking

Now I am sitting
in the new light of sunrise,
thinking old thoughts
and wondering
what I can write today
that is new, and not old,
yet knowing there is nothing
new, that is truly new;
nothing old, that is entirely old.

Eternity

Eternity
is a tabby cat
who stalks the unknowable
by night, then lies all day
in a patch of sun,
vibrating with contentment.

Meditation, with bells . . .

Possessed
of one short and
impermanent life,
the perfect round pings
of the bells, cling
like beaded water to the silence.
One by one,
as if by decision,
they loose themselves
and drop into
the ringing silvery voice
of the singing bowl,
where they disappear entirely,
at-one with
the circle of repetitive touch
which sustains
its music.

E-Mail

You sent me a haiku
on the eve of my 62nd birthday,
a pert little sparrow
that fluttered halfway around the world
and landed,
not one feather out-of-place,
on my shoulder, to sing
this song:

"Sixty-two years of
Wit, grief, anger, joy, laughter
God's truest poem."

Quickly, I launched a little wren
of my own:

"I love you. MOM"

It is easy to see that
even from a world away,
we understand each other
quite well.

Bonsai

It leans into age, as if time
were an agent of grace . . . as if it could,
by the upward curve of its branches,
command an impossible silence of the world.
As I consider how the weight of the absolute
rests lightly among its leaves,
it somehow takes measure of me,
demanding nothing…yet everything.
It resides wholly in the infinity of now,
the ancient and timeless tree,
the beginning, and the end
of forever.

Live

Why linger
in the shadows of life,
braiding together
insubstantial dreams
which can never be carried to light?

Walk out into the fields
where, even now, the morning sun
warms every blade of grass. Accept
your part in this drama.

Be. Do. Love.

Enter into the dwelling
which is God,
by that doorway
which is also God.

Take up your life,
and live.

Only Lacking Words

Opinion lurks
behind my eyes,
unspoken, but not unheard.
Between breaths,
in every cell
of flesh,
I breech thin silence,
only lacking words.

Just for Now

Just for now,
let all accusatory voices
be silent. Let them wander
into some dark wood, where they
lose their way like children
among brambles and berries,
birdsong, and the first blush of morning.
Let them bare their feet to grass,
ponder the life of clouds,
and squeeze a little elemental mud
through their toes.
All in good time, let them return
silent, and ready to open themselves
to even the least of their brothers, knowing
that eternity bends
to the humblest of tasks, and loves
without exception.

Shadows

I love the early morning,
when leaf shadows dance
across the floor,
the house, a quiet garment
with me
at its heart
beating.

St. Paul Farmer's Market

We have come the distance
to be here, bucking traffic for an hour,
then hopping the Green Line from Snelling
into downtown, where we quick-step
along the sidewalk with others heading
the same direction. We have come
to drift down rows of raw color,
among burnt sienna carrots,
slender green slippers of beans,
and the knobbed, snowy pates of cauliflowers
billowing up from tables
like thunderheads in a late summer sky.
In this voluptuous space,
the awe-struck wander like voyeurs
among sun-warmed purple eggplants,
buckets of rough-skinned beets, and the
juicy round udders of red and gold tomatoes;
touching . . . squeezing . . . lifting them up
and holding them to the light like crisp jewels.
The dark-eyed, tolerant growers smile
and exude a seasoned confidence.
What price for such treasure? A mere
three dollars per tray. Like honey bees,
mad for summer's last sweetness,
we alight everywhere,
unable to make up our minds.

The Pessimist

He stands
Over the watermelon,
Well-honed knife in hand,
And divides its sweet red flesh
Into precisely-cut pieces,
Complaining all the while
Of its many dark seeds.

The Greening Life
a sonnet inspired by green beans

Whose calloused fingers reached to harvest these
Beneath the sun-warmed leaves, their blossomed
  stalks?
Bewildered by the rasp of human talk,
He sought a place where man may take his ease
Among the shining rows of waving beans,
Stepped in, then knelt, and felt along their stems
For every slender, meaty, rain-crisped gem,
And plucked himself a bucket full of green.
Perhaps as evening fell, as cricket choirs
Filled up the night, he sat upon the step
To ponder seed and stalk, the greening life,
To break and wash, then set them to the fire,
Where now, they simmer like a promise kept
Beneath the knowing smile of his dear wife.

No One Knows

They toil no more along the rows
To rise, and ripple . . . bloom, and fruit.
Of late, my garden's bounty froze,

And so I gathered in the beans,
Withheld them from the greedy crows
Who scavenge there for what remains.

They simmer now atop my stove,
This stolen cache of emerald loot,
And why I picked them, no one knows.

Haiku

slender green slippers
some careless elf walks barefoot
lost among the rows

break their crisp hearts
the secret of their greenness
weeping in your hands

Ode to Words

To the way they gather excitedly
at the doorway
of my consciousness
whispering
and milling about
until I come to touch the latch
and open. To the rush
of their inpouring, and the
open-handed gifts they bring.
To the way they frisk and play,
first lining up as expected,
then bursting ranks
and reassembling into
something I never dreamed.
To the poem, which is
their final flowering
and fruit.

To whatever ancient
and understanding Soul
still considers me
worthy.

Clip Clop

Broad of back, and dappled gray,
with hooves the size of pie plates,
he leans into the leather harness
like a pro, clip-clopping along
narrow Charleston streets
where fire, and the Civil War
have more-than-once
burned the city to the ground.
Steady as an old war horse,
he nods his blinkered head
to the beat of steel shoes on cement,
and patiently walks the familiar route,
stopping where he should stop,
turning where he should turn.
With grace, and in spite of
what may or may not have happened
those long years ago, he delivers up
his carriage full of Yankees
to the safety of the barn,
where they clamber down and out,
emptying it
of their clipped conversations,
their hurried Northern ways.

Two Men in a Boat

Out early,
they float along the edge
of a silence broken only
by the loneliness
of one loon calling to another.
Cradled in mist, their weathered keel
rides the water
like a forgotten bobber
half-submerged
in a simpler time and place.
They have cast their lines
into the thick gray soup of morning
and now they wait, without conversation,
for a fish to rise.

There is no way to tell
whether the slow burning-off of fog
will find them
still fishing, and hopeful
or resigned to failure,
and gone.

Buffalo

They wandered, thick as unplowed prairie grass
And dark as earth,
Nosing the flanks of tawny bawling calves
Still fresh from birth,
And poured the thunder of a thousand hooves
Betwixt the turf
Of undivided plain, and guileless sky,
Imparting worth
To endless miles of empty wind-swept land,
O'er centuries unmarred by greedy hands.

Badlands Meditation

Shouldering up
through the grassy flank of South Dakota,
the long-buried past
lies bare as an open wound
through which ancient warriors
thrust the battle-scarred crags of their faces,
and dark-eyed women recline
against grass-furred prairies,
watching the eternal drift of clouds
across the sky.

After eons,
their bodies still flare
with the colors of a once-vibrant life.
What remains
sifts slowly away into time,
adrift in the restless prairie wind, trickling
down the face of the weathered hills
like tears.

Small wonder
our voices fall silent,
not wanting to wake them…not wanting
them to see
how we wander so lost
where dark clouds of buffalo
once pummeled the land
like thunder.

Blackbird

A lone blackbird, silently
Winging its way
Across pale morning,
Lifted my eyes toward the
Deep, hollow bowl of the sky
Whose upended basin
Pours
From impossible depths,
An ardent blue attention
Across the threshold of daily life,
However small, ordinary,
Or uninspired
We may consider it
To be.

Lily

Oh, look!
Some invisible hand
Has loosened
The long buttery petals
Of the tall lily. Their
Velveteen bodies
Drop, without complaint
From the steep spiral stair
Of green swords.

Fallen,
They resemble
A scattered yellow reflection
Of the original bloom.
Excepting, of course,
That small
Imperceptible
Sigh
Of grief.

Morning

Light walks a slender thread
across air.
Morning is reborn,
a spider's silk
connecting light
to life.

The Question

The fox lay perfectly still
In the russet, black-gloved gown of his body,
Its burnished silk lifting a little in the breeze
Like waving grass. He seemed almost
To glow, although life's spark had flown
And his eyes were full of death.

Across the cornfield, in a gnarl of oaks,
Crows rasped at the rising sun. Soon,
They'd discover and plunder his body,
Leaving only a scatter of bones and fur.
And life
Would simply go on.

Standing there, I wondered:
Why must even the brave die?
The sly, the crafty, the beautiful,
Each in their turn? But no answer came.
Only the thrum and whir of insects, and
An occasional car, humming along blacktop.

And so, I walked on home, and left
My question with eternity, where it belongs.
For I knew with certainty that all across the
meadow,
Wherever this fox had roamed,
Scampering, soft-bodied creatures
Were rejoicing.

Dusk

Impacted blue,
The heavy dusk
Descends, its rim
Bedecked with rust.

Through coral clouds
That darken so,
Relentlessly
Its forces flow,

And bowl us over
Head to heel,
That ancient, whole,
And un-cleaved wheel.

Doorstep

In and out of sleep
all night,
I kept waking
to the virtuoso performance
of a single brown cricket.

From his first-chair position
in the pit beneath the doorstep,
he leaned into
every pure note, drawing
his long bow across the body
of his high-pitched fiddle,
quite unable
to lay this essential music down
and take a final bow.

While I Slept

While I slept
the black cat of night
padded silently in
and curled itself around my dreams.

It watched awhile
with great yellow eyes,
and then bounded quietly over
the edge of the world,
chasing fireflies
and stars.

Our Reticulate Self

This space we occupy,
    this grace
    this given.
Scaffold of bones. Blossom
of flesh. Tributaries of blood.
Borders of skin, calloused
    with too much touch,
    tender with too little.
Windowed. Out-facing.
In-taking. Breath by breath,
    our reticulate self.

More Human

This thought remains,
  a remedy of sorts.
That we stood apart, yet knew
that we were one. That we
understood what was impossible,
but risked hoping it was not.
That, of hope and love
and something else unnamed,
we became more human
than we had yet been.
That we nested, one bowl
of worry or hurt or craziness,
into the other, and that life, with its
clinging residues of acid and sweet,
somehow achieved,
of our sharing,
a balance.

Wisdom

It fills us slowly,
like snowfall sifts
against a distant mountain,
solidifying over eons
into blue glacial ice.
No one asks
why it takes so long
for this ponderous concrete river
to reach the sea.
It will arrive, unhurried,
in its own sweet time.

So too, the conviction
that love trumps hate,
that life is a schoolhouse
as well as a cathedral,
and that when you plant a garden,
your hands often get dirty.

Light

Light comes walking
With its silent questions.
Morning
Is gray with dew.
Here, at the east window,
The long legs and delicate wings
Of a crane fly
Are holding up the sky.

A Promise Kept

Another cold flint morning
unfurls
in the warmth
of its own bright spark.
The sun rises
like a promise kept,
and darkness slinks away
to the borders of light.

About the Author

Sharon K Sheppard has been writing poetry for over 30 years. Her roots are set firmly in the midwestern states of Iowa, South Dakota, and Minnesota. She enjoyed a long and happy career in the paper industry. Sharon is the grateful mother of two sons, and grandmother to four children who never stop surprising her. She resides with her husband in Isanti, Minnesota.

CPSIA information can be obtained
at www.ICGtesting.com
Printed in the USA
LVHW112139201222
735671LV00022B/314

9 781511 957205